THE PHILLIP KEVEREN SERIES   EASY PIANO

SWEET LAND OF LIBERTY

CONTENTS

— PIANO LEVEL —
EARLY INTERMEDIATE
(HLSPL LEVEL 4-5)

ISBN 978-0-634-04369-7

7777 W. BLUEMOUND RD. P.O. BOX 13819 MILWAUKEE, WI 53213

Visit Hal Leonard Online at
www.halleonard.com

PREFACE

Sweet Land of Liberty was written in the weeks following September 11, 2001. Although we always had intended to include a patriotic folio in this series, plans were not yet definite. A lot of things changed for all of us on that tragic Tuesday.

I was preparing to present a workshop to piano teachers in Colorado Springs when the news flashed across the television. As I continued my journey by rental car across the heartland of America that week, I was deeply moved by the music I heard on the radio. "America, the Beautiful" seemed to resonate deeper than ever before in my life. The National Cathedral service that Friday included "The Battle Hymn of the Republic", and it was the most powerful rendering I'd heard in many years.

I began writing the settings for *Sweet Land of Liberty* (and its Piano Solo companion, *Let Freedom Ring!*) that very week. It became part of a healing process for me. As I studied the music and texts of these treasured songs, I became even more grateful for the freedom with which we have been blessed.

My sincere prayer is that these arrangements will draw you into a greater appreciation of the rich heritage we share as Americans. "My country, 'tis of thee, sweet land of liberty, of thee I sing!"

With a grateful heart,
Phillip Keveren

BIOGRAPHY

Phillip Keveren, a multi-talented keyboard artist and composer, has composed original works in a variety of genres from piano solo to symphonic orchestra. Mr. Keveren gives frequent concerts and workshops for teachers and their students in the United States, Canada, Europe, and Asia. Mr. Keveren holds a B.M. in composition from California State University Northridge and a M.M. in composition from the University of Southern California.

AMERICA, THE BEAUTIFUL

Words by KATHERINE LEE BATES
Music by SAMUEL A. WARD
Arranged by Phillip Keveren

Moderately slow, expressively

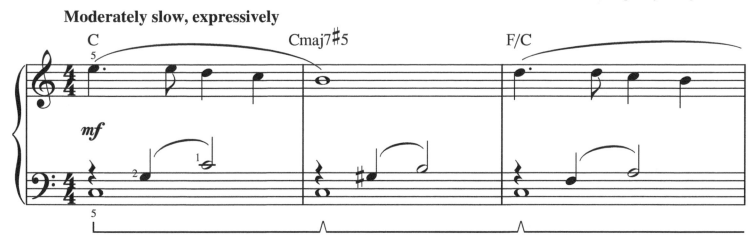

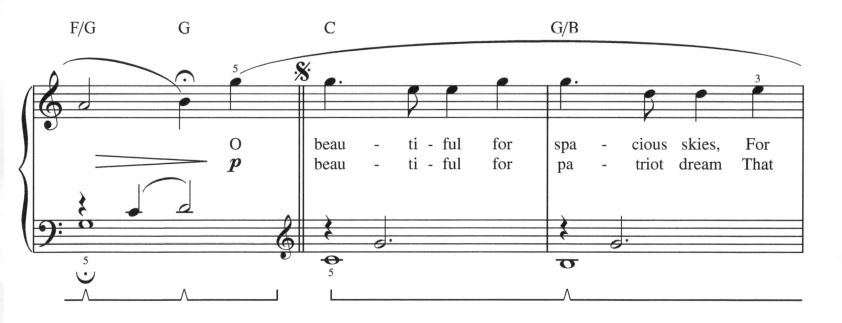

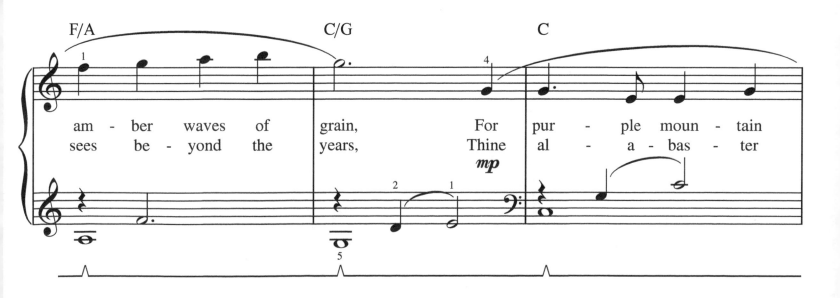

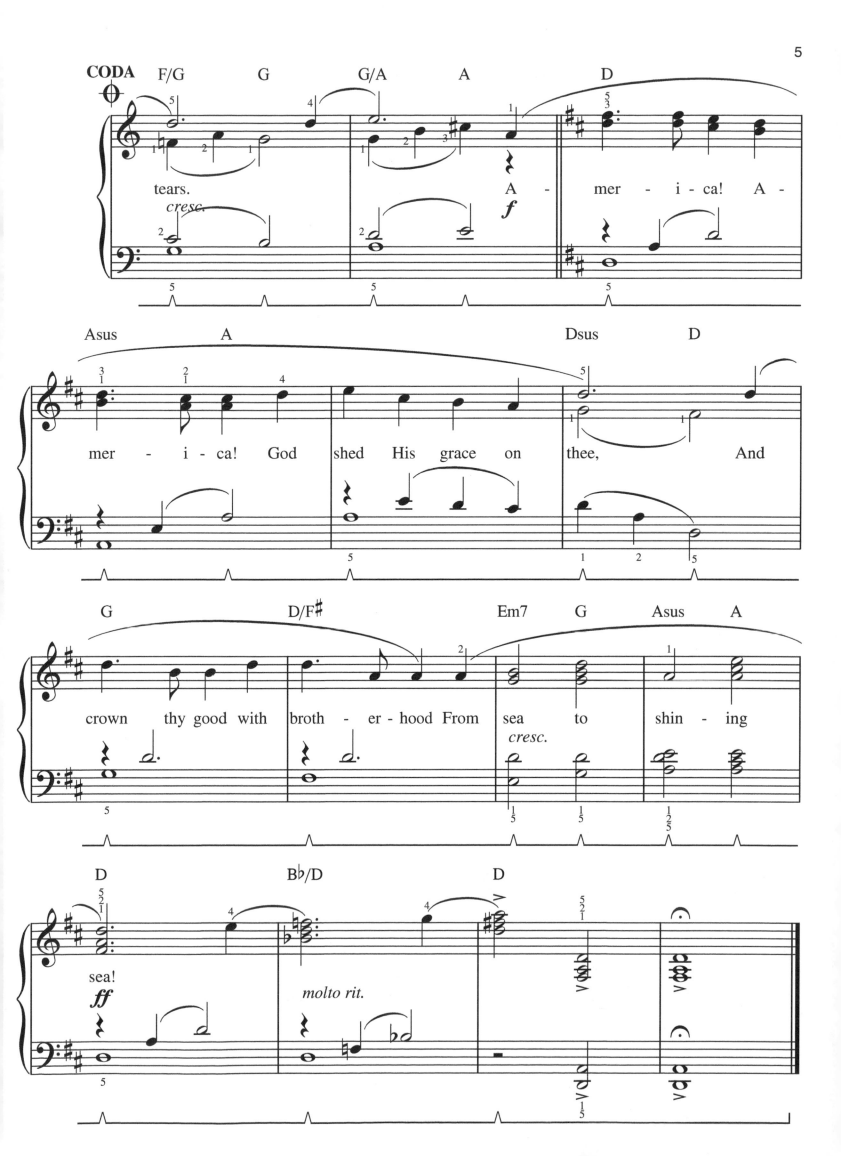

5

ANCHORS AWEIGH

Words by ALFRED HART MILES and ROYAL LOVELL
Music by CHARLES A. ZIMMERMAN
Additional Lyrics by GEORGE D. LOTTMAN
Arranged by Phillip Keveren

Bright March

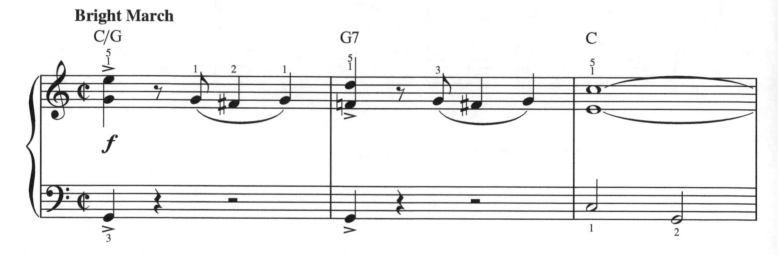

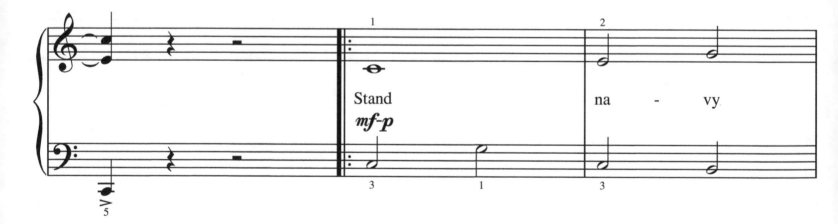

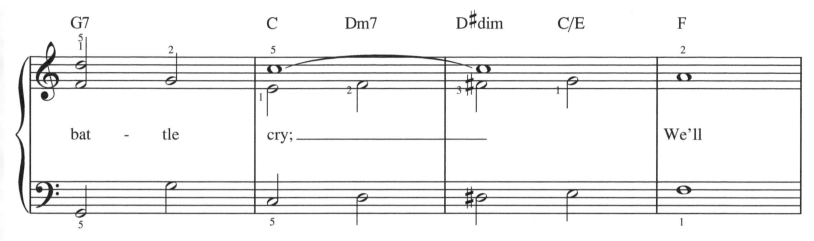

bat - tle cry; _____ We'll

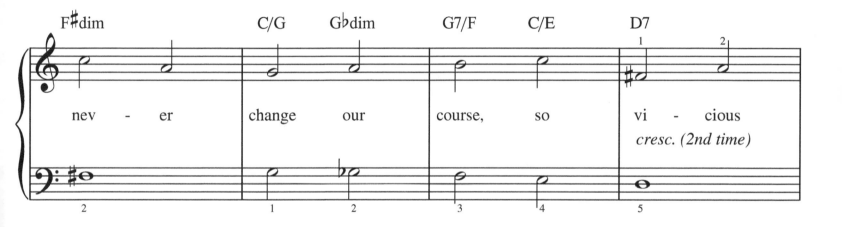

nev - er change our course, so vi - cious
cresc. (2nd time)

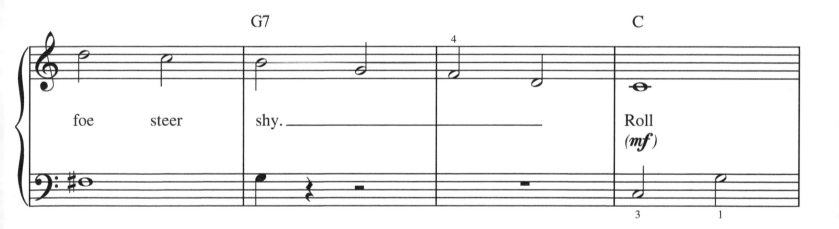

foe steer shy. _____ Roll
*(**mf**)*

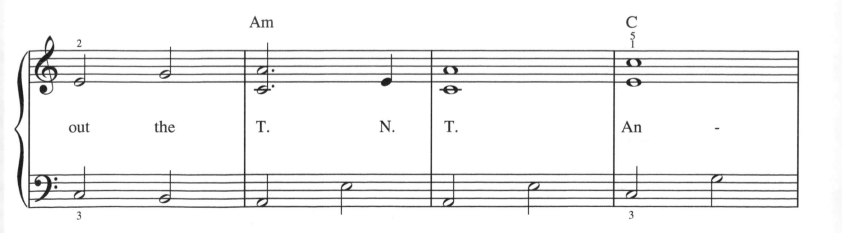

out the T. N. T. An -

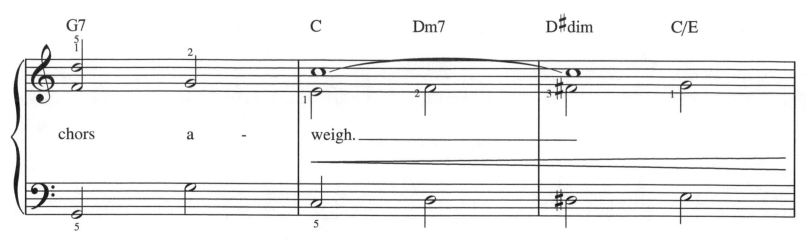

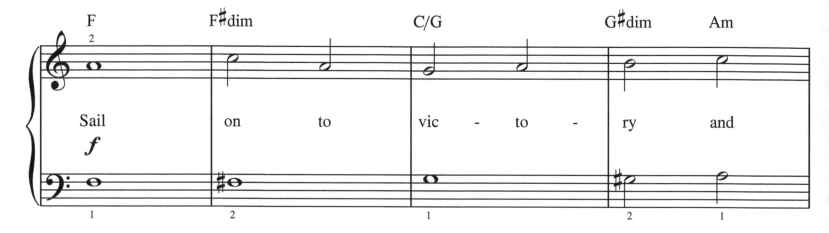

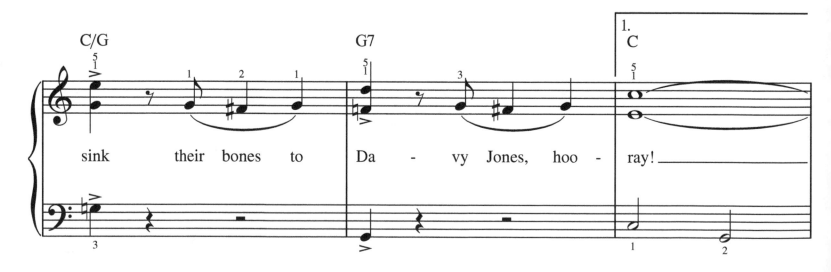

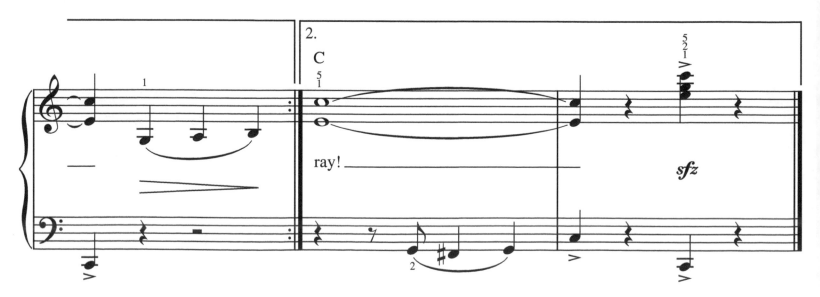

BATTLE HYMN OF THE REPUBLIC

Words by JULIA WARD HOWE
Music by WILLIAM STEFFE
Arranged by Phillip Keveren

Slowly, stately

eyes have seen the glo-ry of the com-ing of the Lord, He is tramp-ling out the vin-tage where the grapes of wrath are stored; He hath

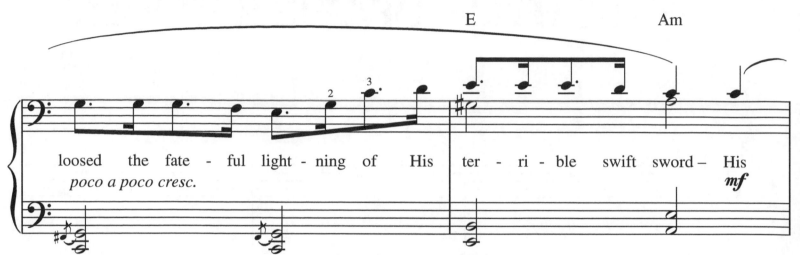

loosed the fate - ful light - ning of His ter - ri - ble swift sword — His
poco a poco cresc.

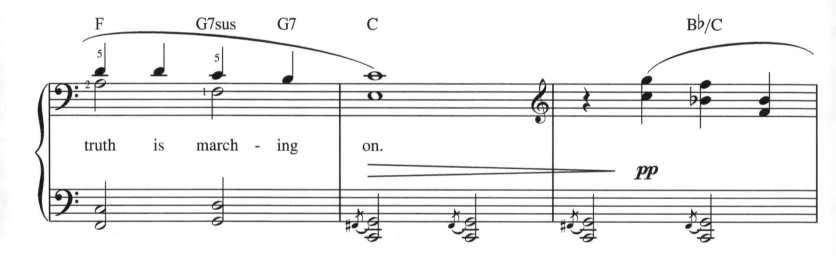

truth is march - ing on.

Glo - ry! glo - ry, hal - le - lu - jah!

Glo - ry! glo - ry, hal - le - lu - jah!

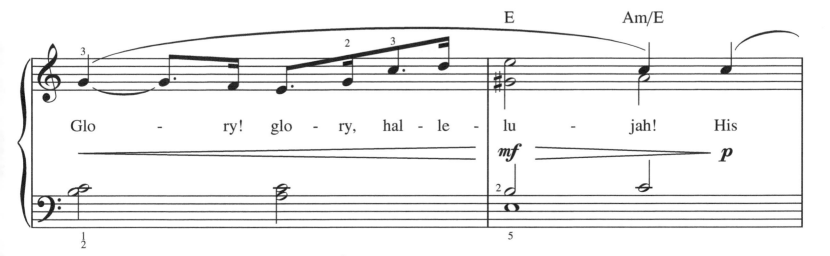

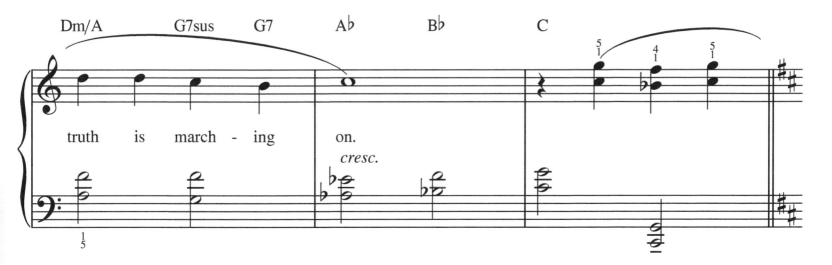

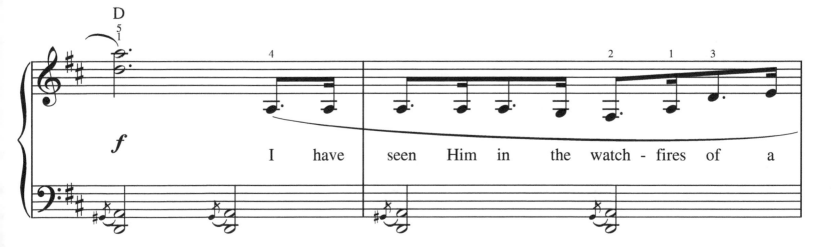

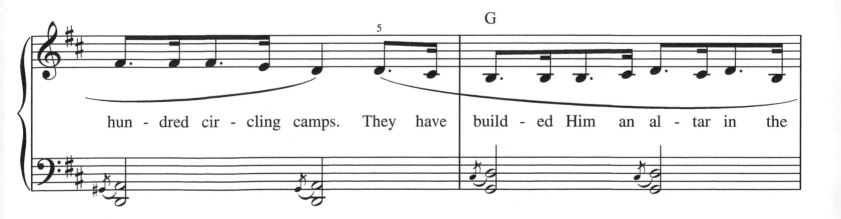

eve - ning dews and damps; I can read His right - eous sen - tence by the

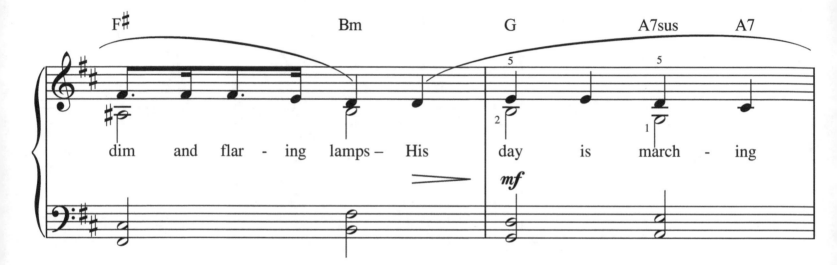

dim and flar - ing lamps— His day is march - ing

on. Glo - ry! glo - ry, hal - le -

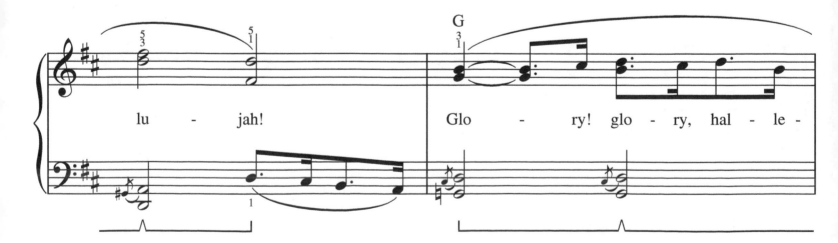

lu - jah! Glo - ry! glo - ry, hal - le -

lu - jah! Glo - ry! glo - ry, hal - le - lu - jah! His

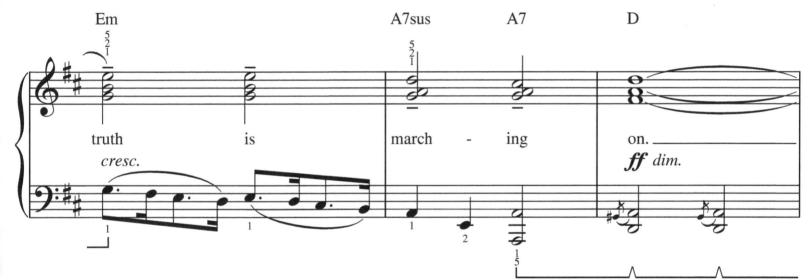

truth is march - ing on.

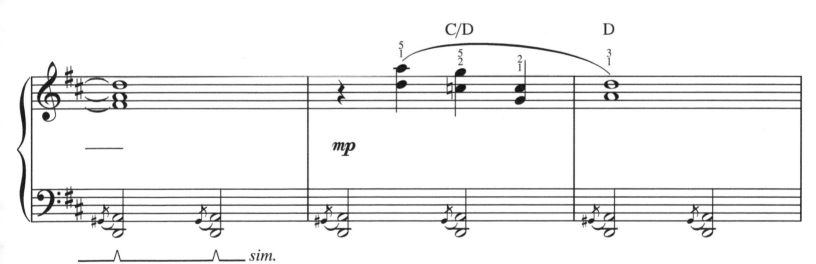

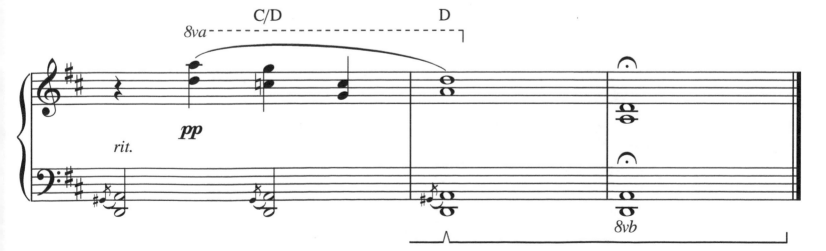

ETERNAL FATHER, STRONG TO SAVE

Words by WILLIAM WHITING
Music by JOHN BACCHUS DYKES
Arranged by Phillip Keveren

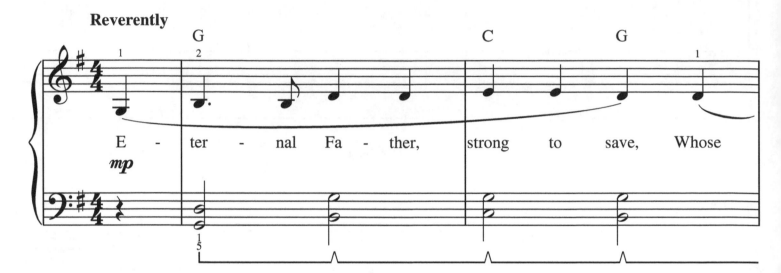

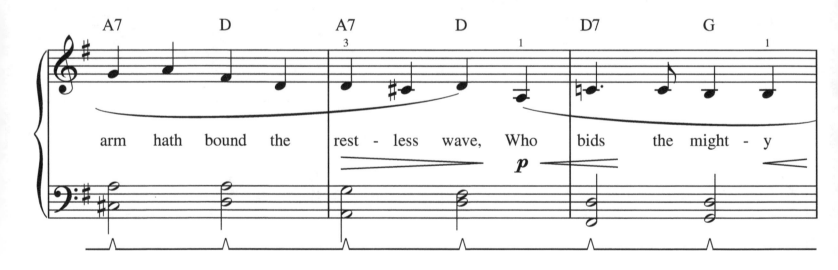

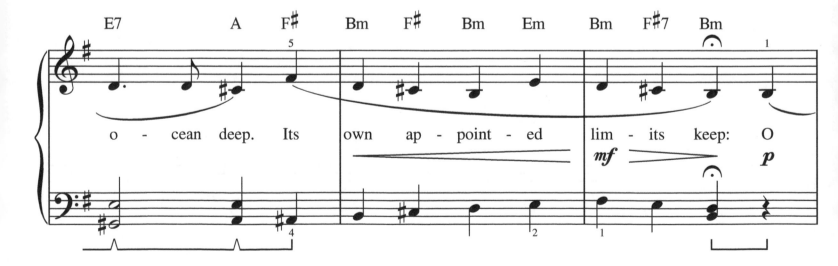

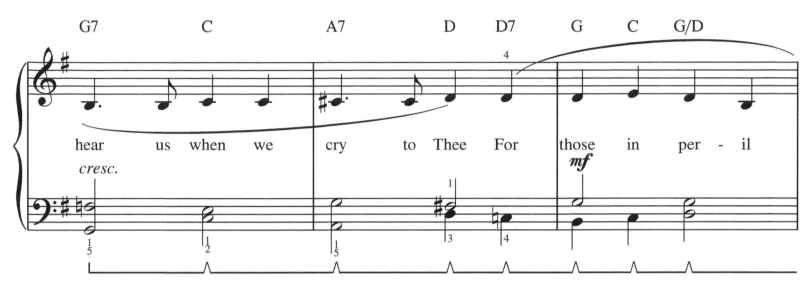

Slower, with strength

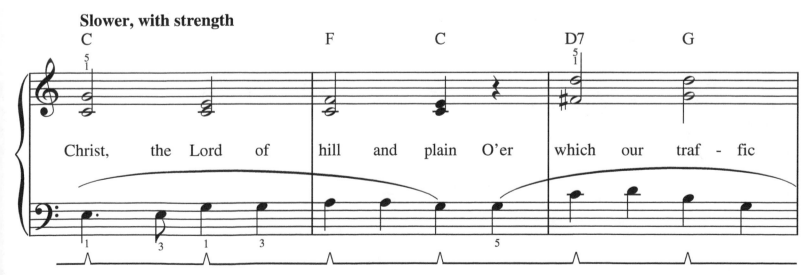

GOD OF OUR FATHERS

Words by DANIEL CRANE ROBERTS
Music by GEORGE WILLIAM WARREN
Arranged by Phillip Keveren

With fanfare

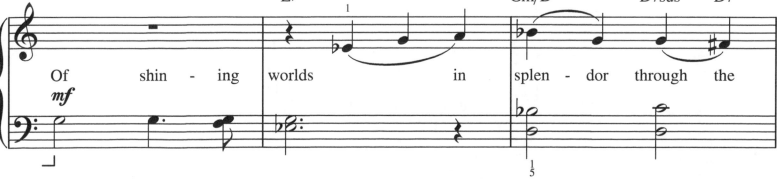

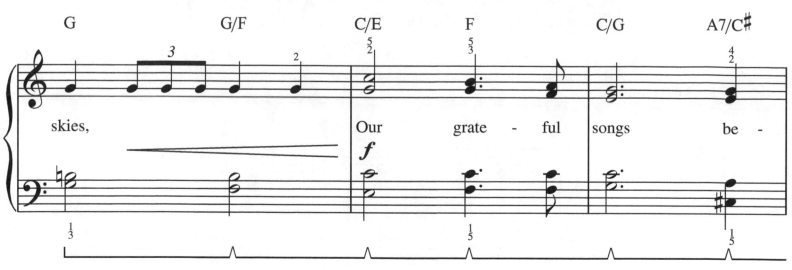

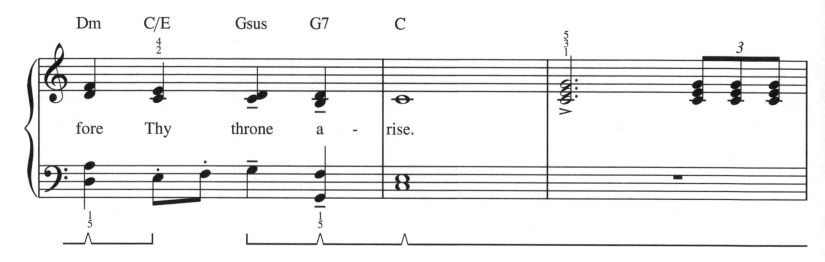

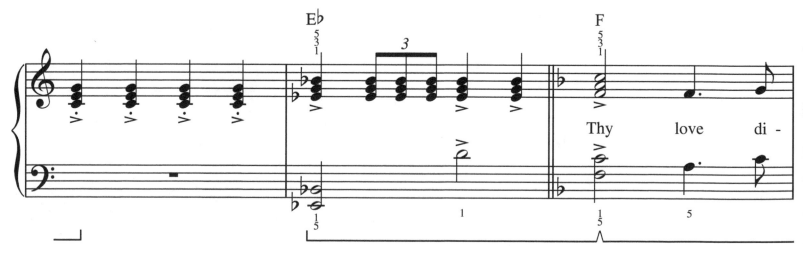

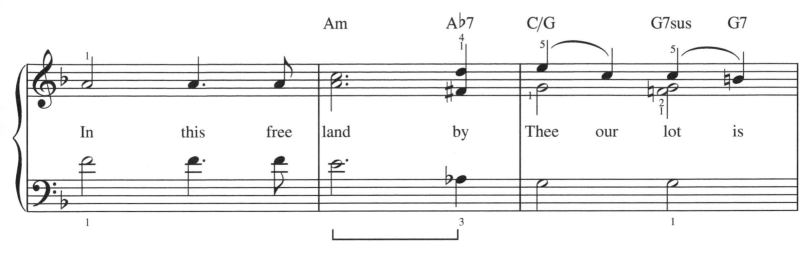

In this free land by Thee our lot is

cast; Be Thou our Rul - er,

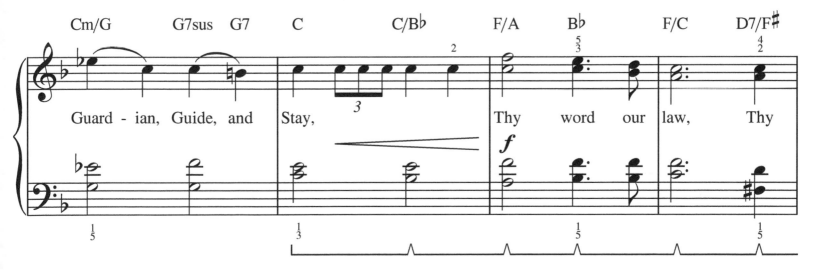

Guard - ian, Guide, and Stay, Thy word our law, Thy

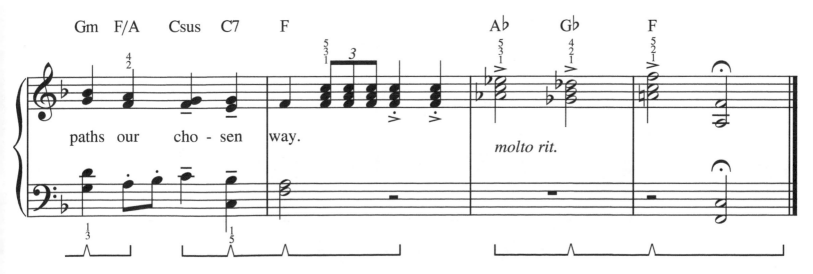

paths our cho - sen way.

GOD BLESS OUR NATIVE LAND

Traditional
Arranged by Phillip Keveren

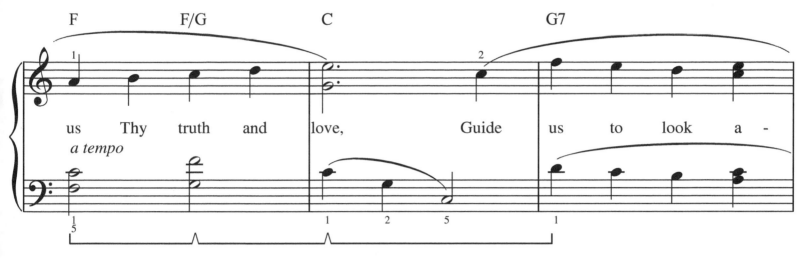

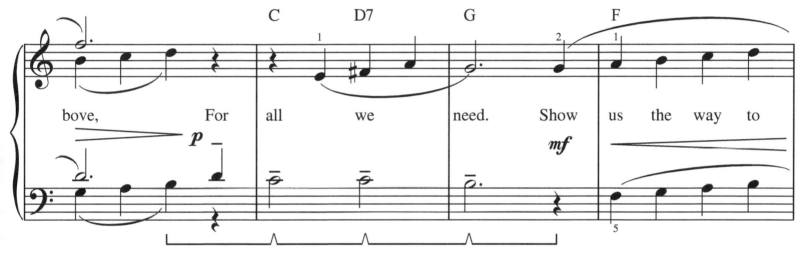

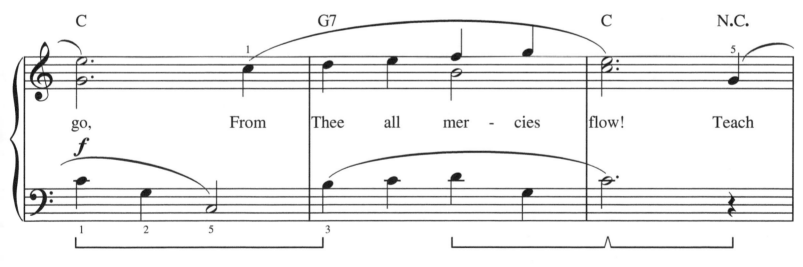

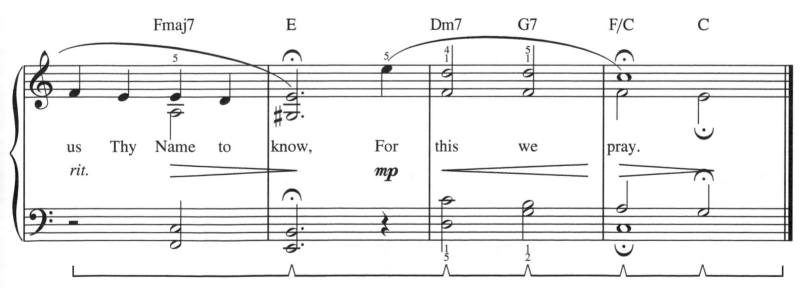

HAIL TO THE CHIEF

By JAMES SANDERSON
Arranged by Phillip Keveren

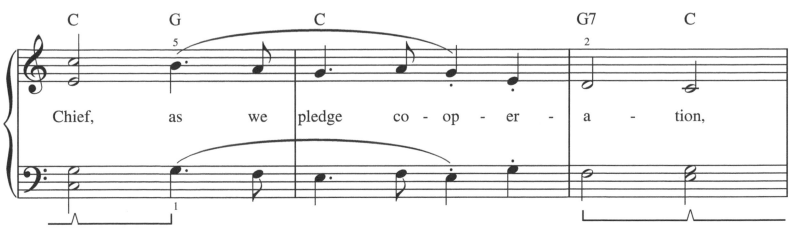

Chief, as we pledge co-op-er-a-tion,

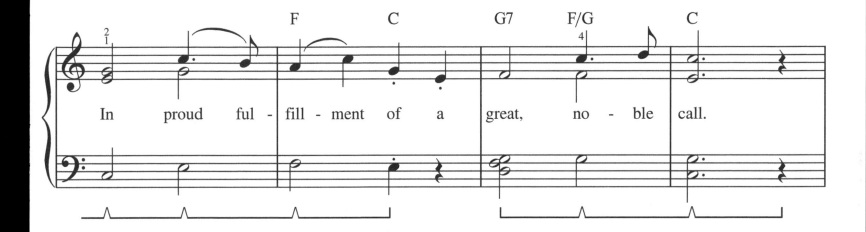

In proud ful-fill-ment of a great, no-ble call.

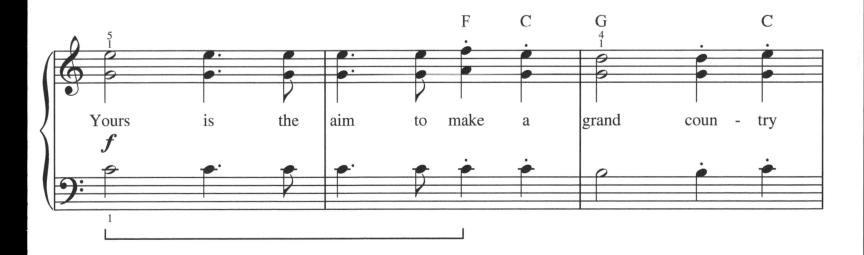

Yours is the aim to make a grand coun-try

f

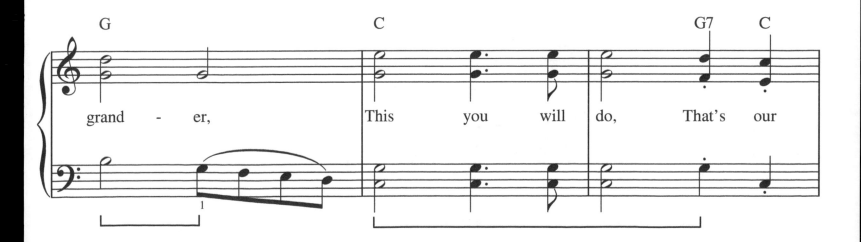

grand-er, This you will do, That's our

strong,   firm   be - lief.   Hail   to   the

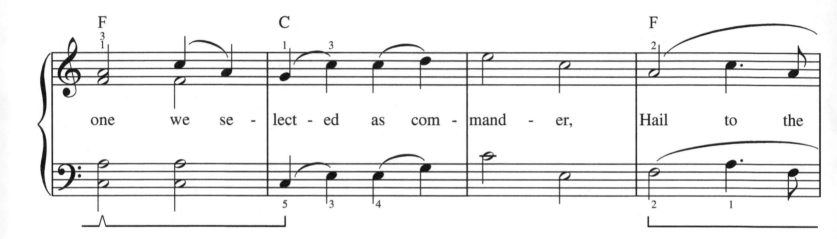

one   we   se - lect - ed   as   com - mand - er,   Hail   to   the

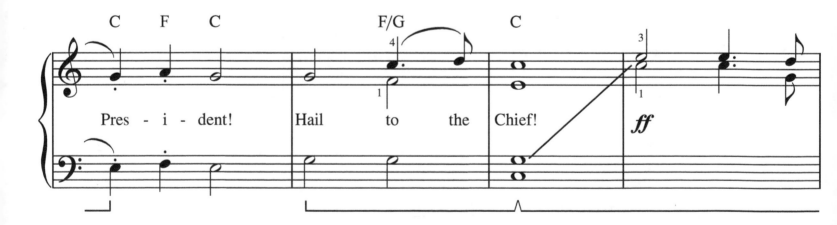

Pres - i - dent!   Hail   to   the   Chief!   *ff*

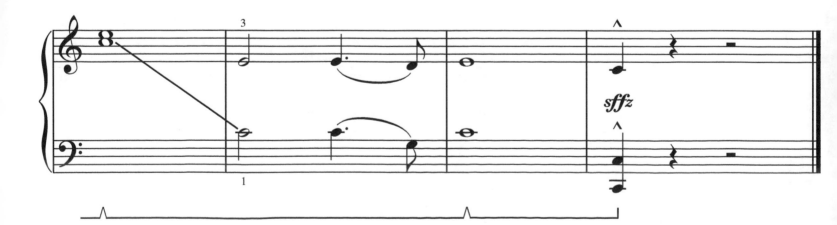

sffz

THE STAR SPANGLED BANNER

Words by FRANCIS SCOTT KEY
Music by JOHN STAFFORD SMITH
Arranged by Phillip Keveren

With fanfare

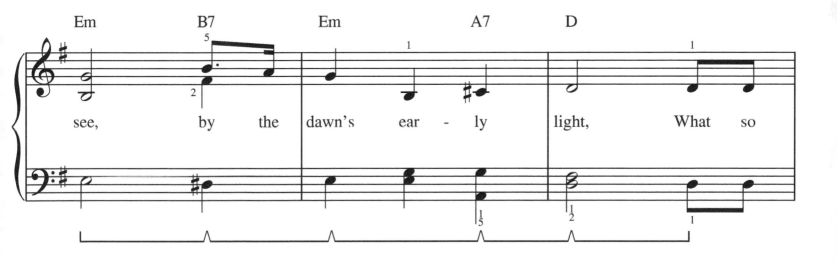

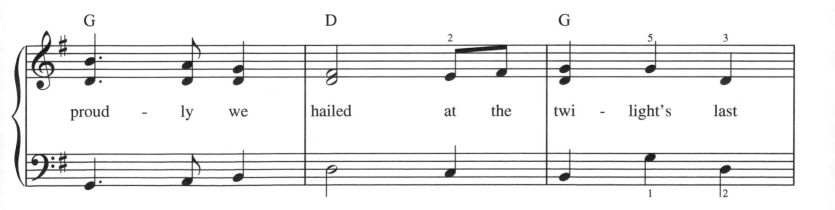

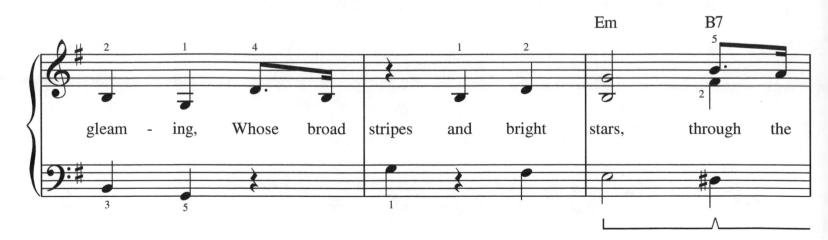

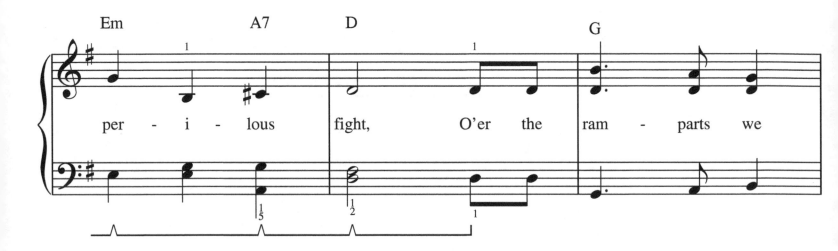

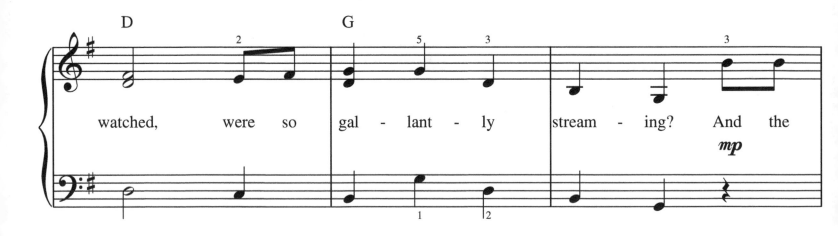

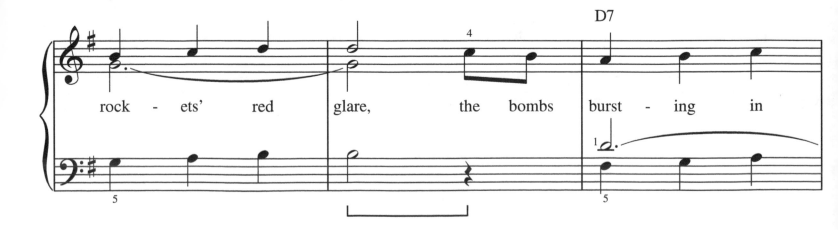

27

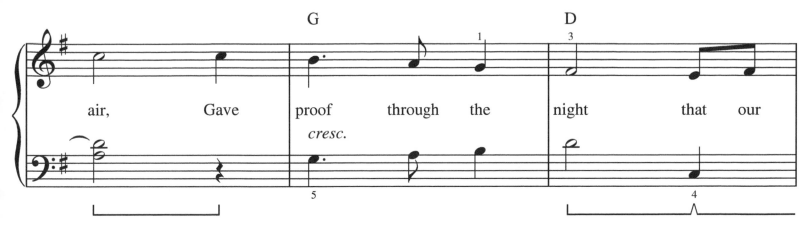

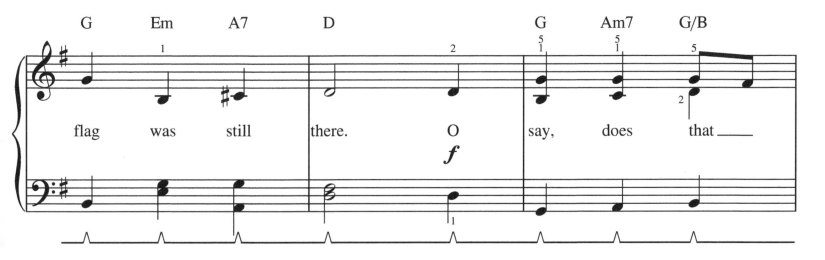

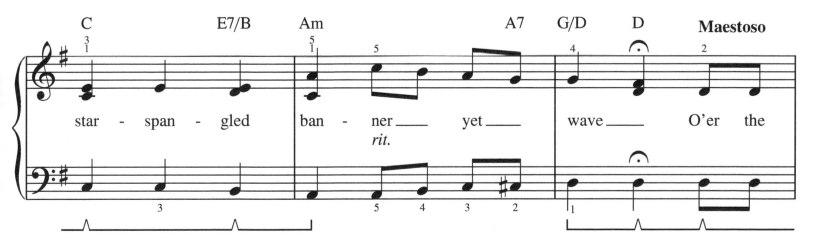

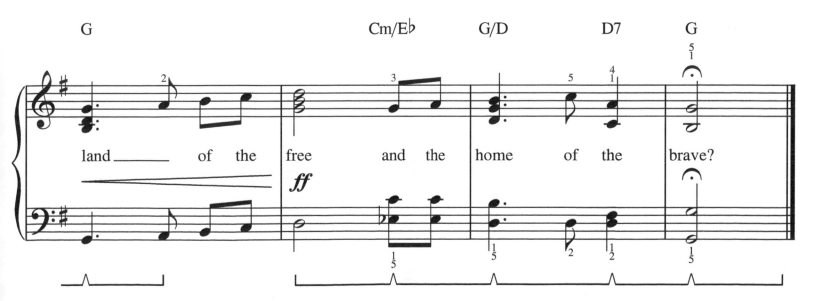

MY COUNTRY, 'TIS OF THEE
(America)

Words by SAMUEL FRANCIS SMITH
Music from *Thesaurus Musicus*
Arranged by Phillip Keveren

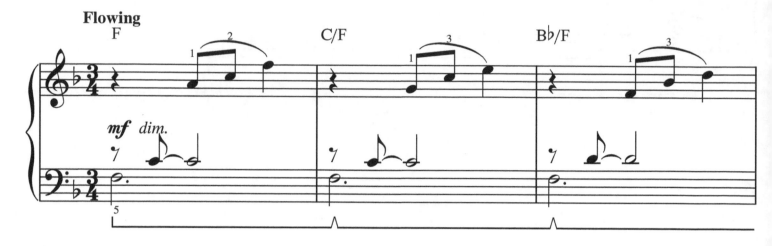

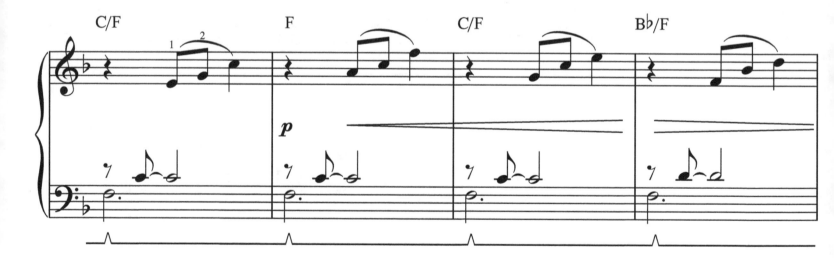

My coun - try 'tis of thee,

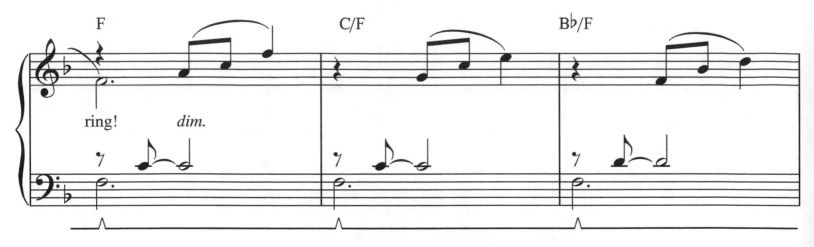

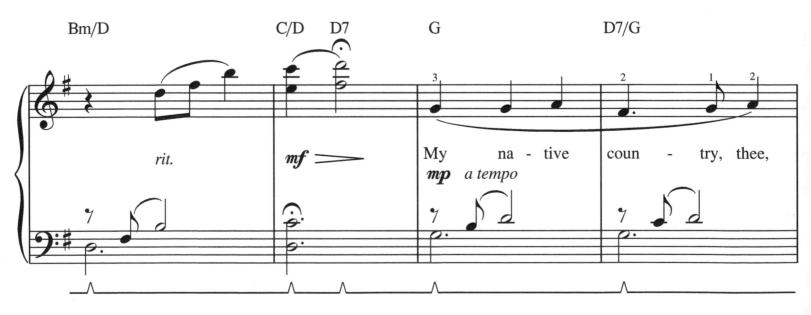

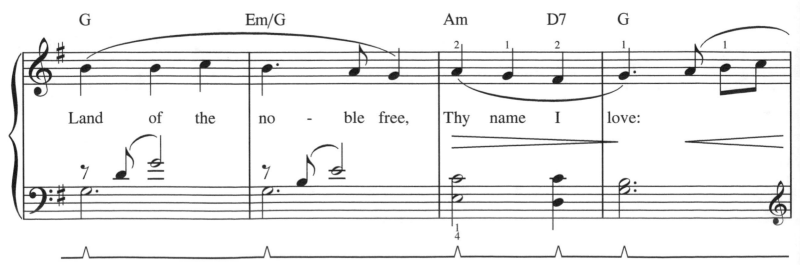

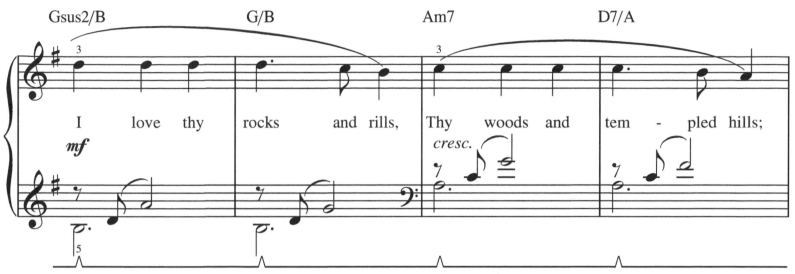

I love thy rocks and rills, Thy woods and tem - pled hills;

mf
cresc.

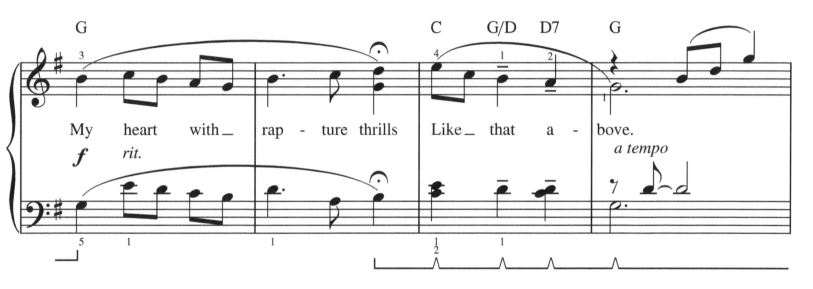

My heart with rap - ture thrills Like that a - bove.

f *rit.*
a tempo

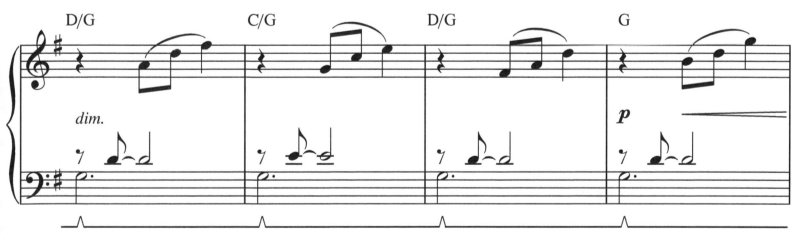

dim.

p

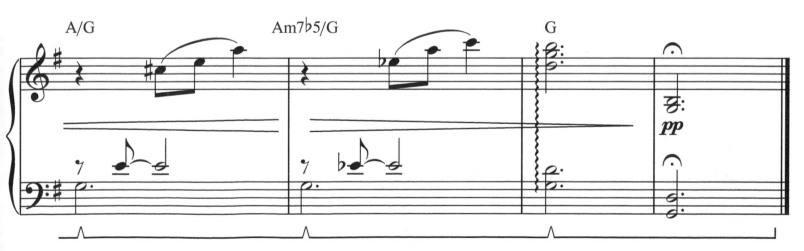

pp

SEMPER FIDELIS

By JOHN PHILIP SOUSA
Arranged by Phillip Keveren

Bright March (in two)

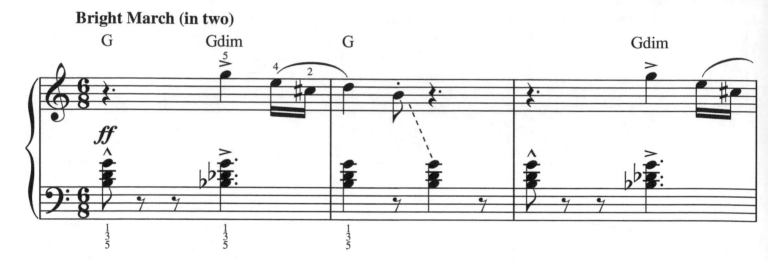

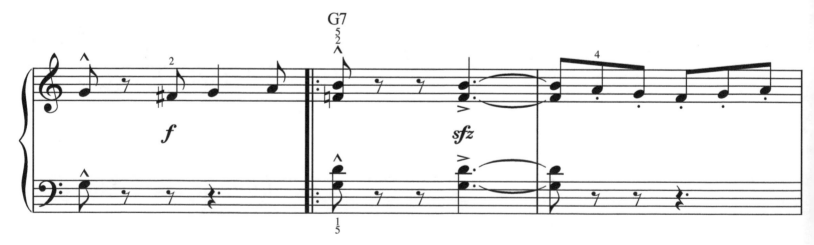

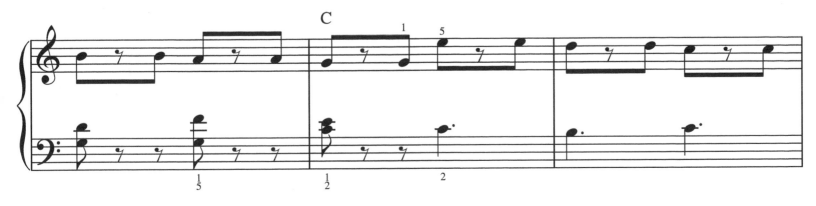

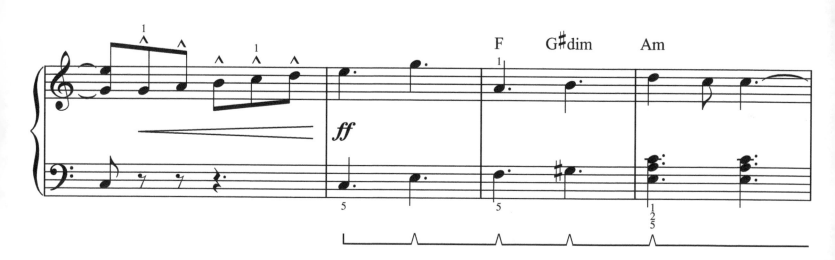

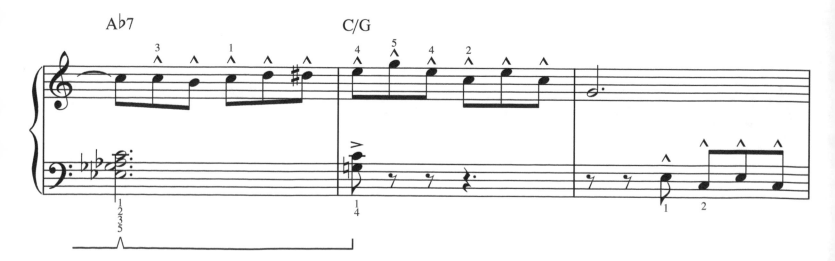

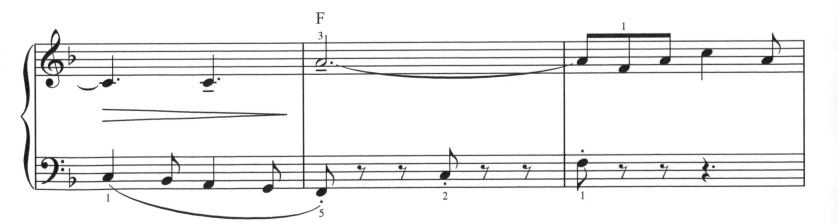

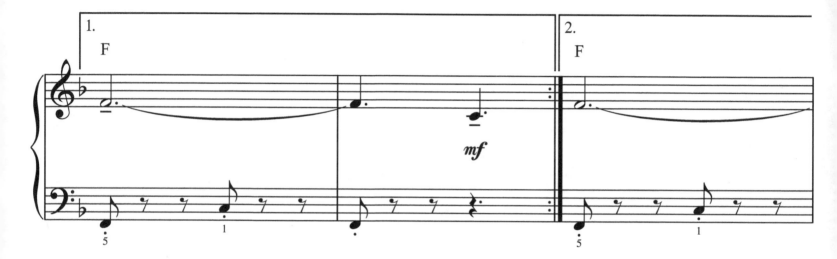

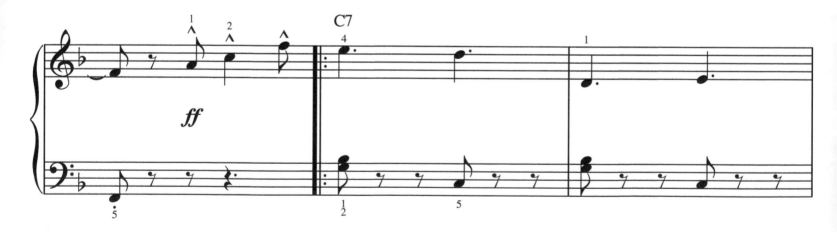

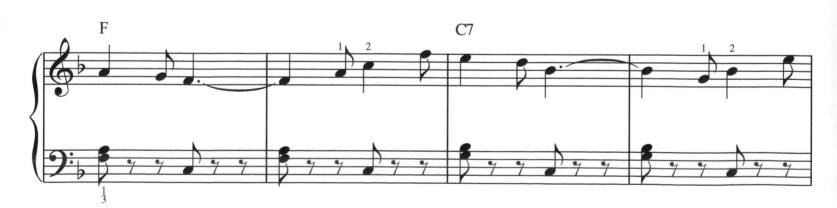

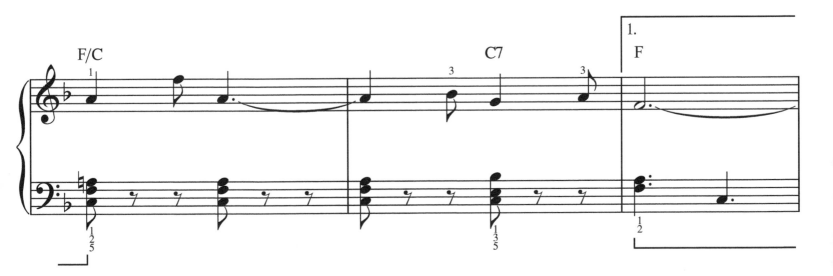

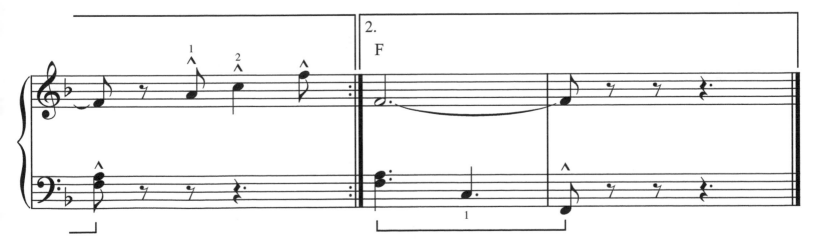

STARS AND STRIPES FOREVER

By JOHN PHILIP SOUSA
Arranged by Phillip Keveren

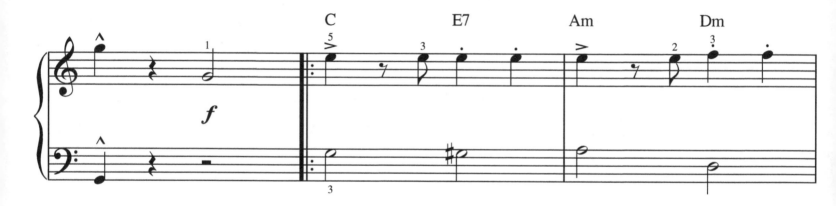

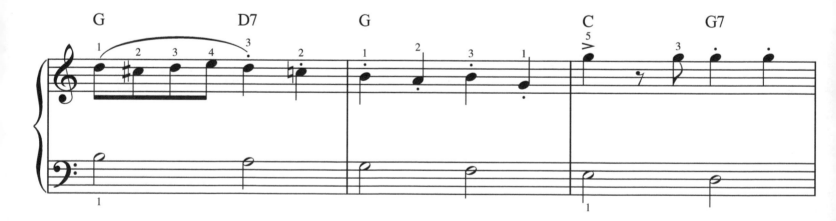

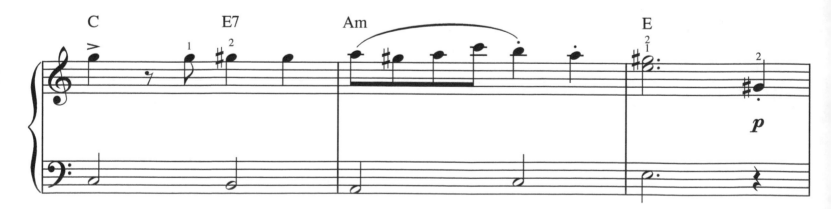

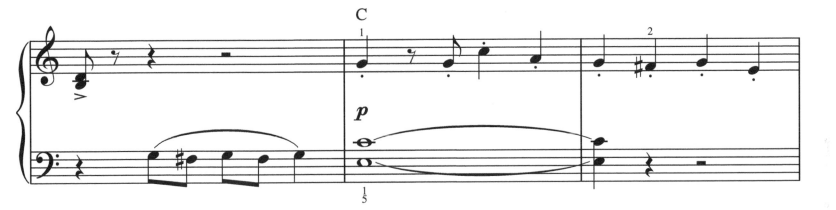

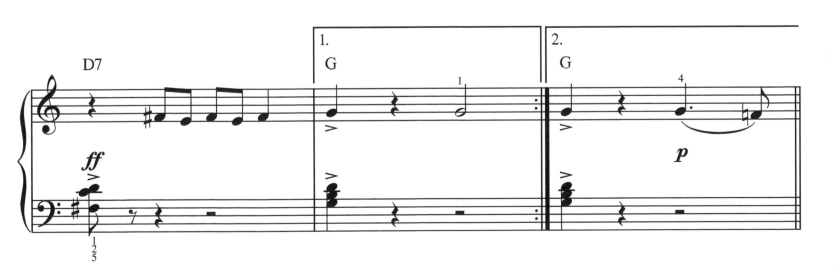

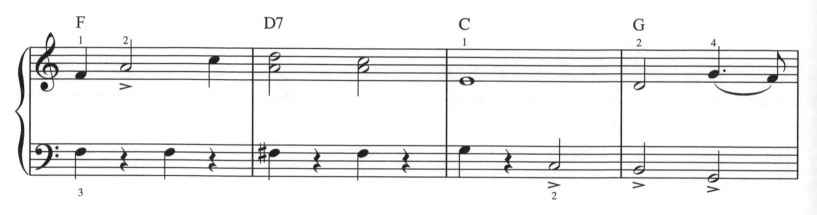

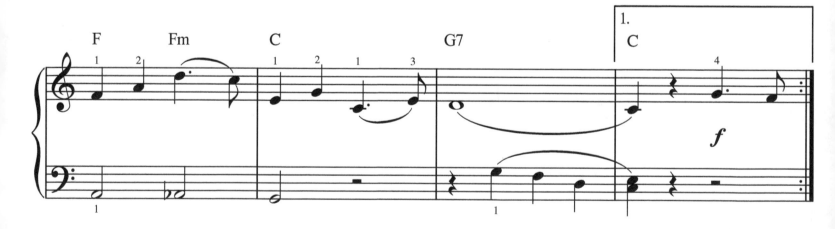

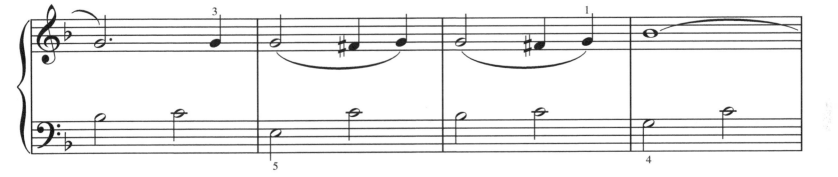

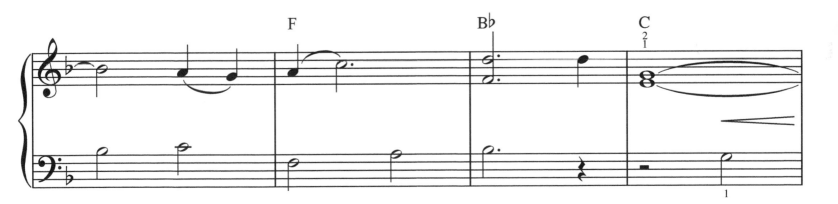

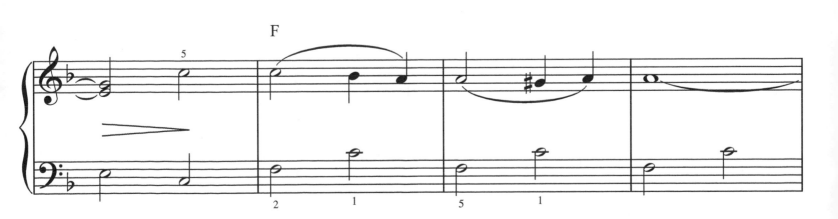

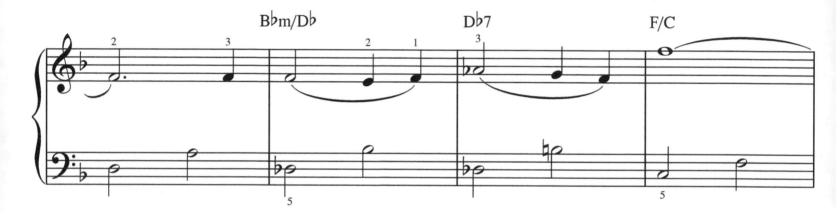

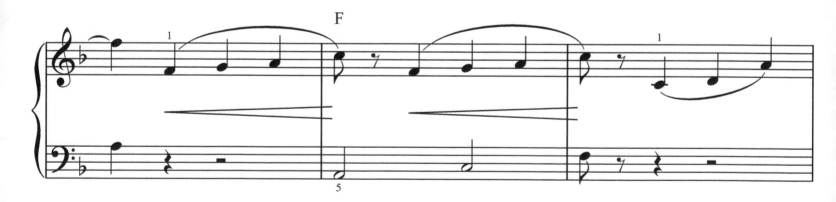

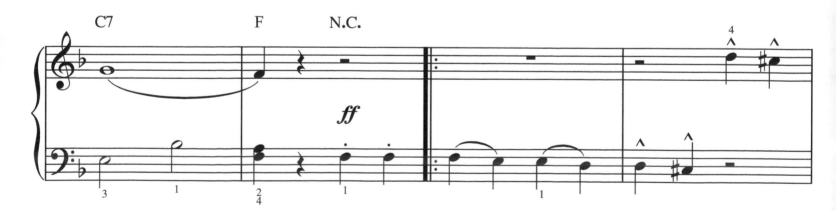

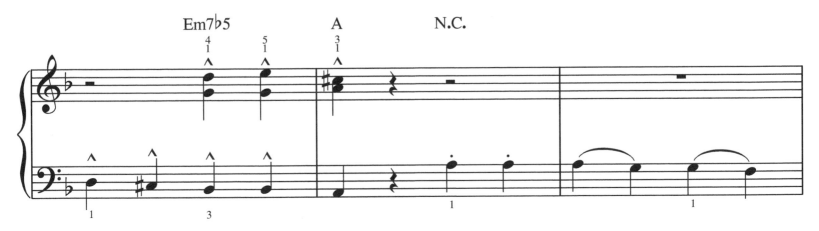

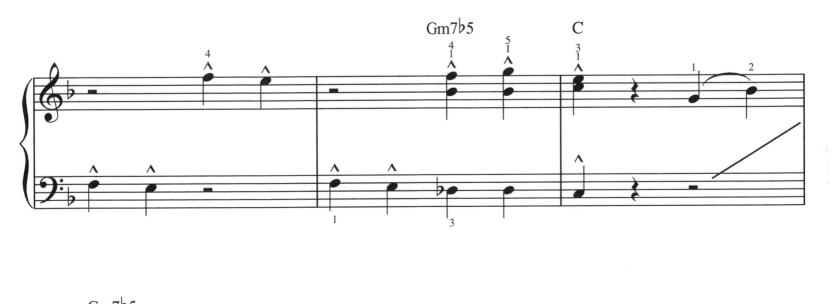

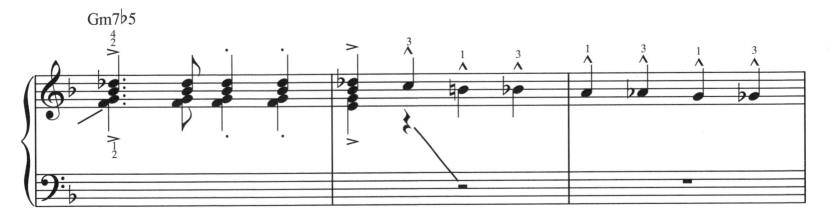

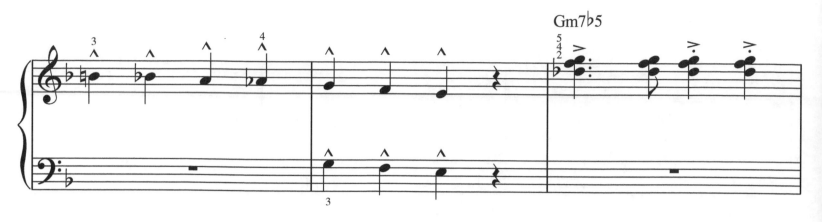

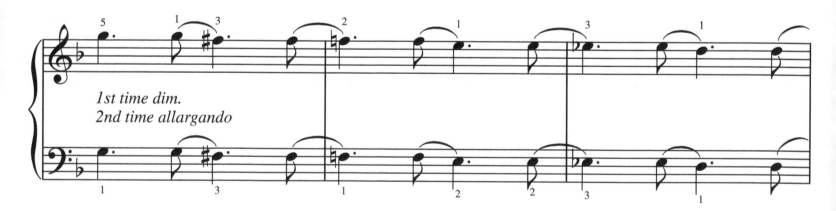

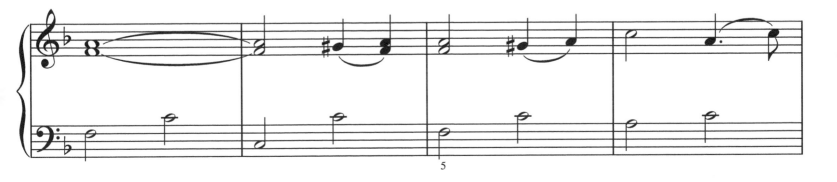

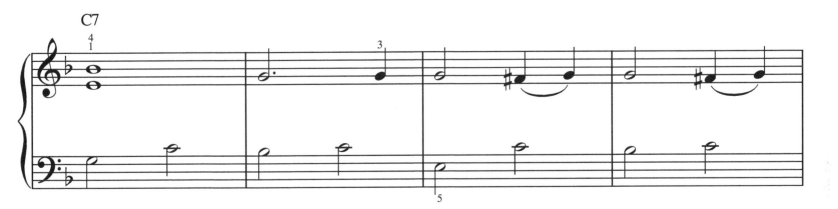

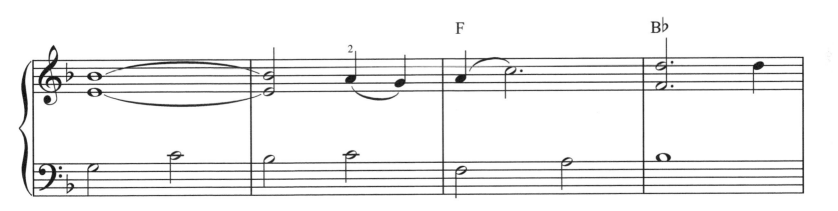

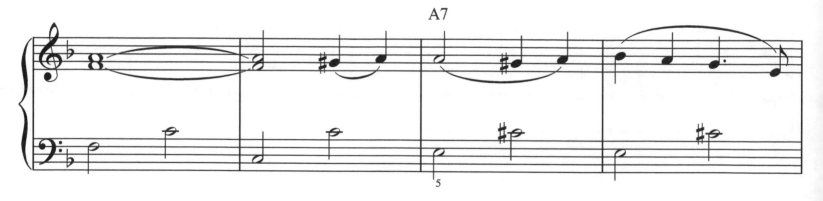

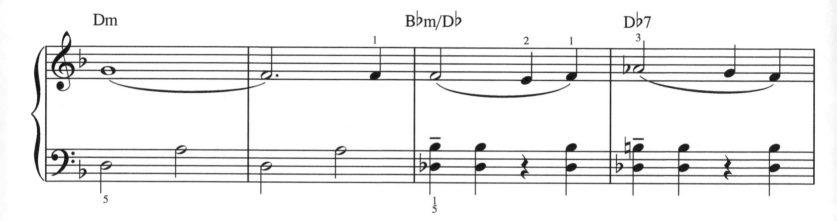

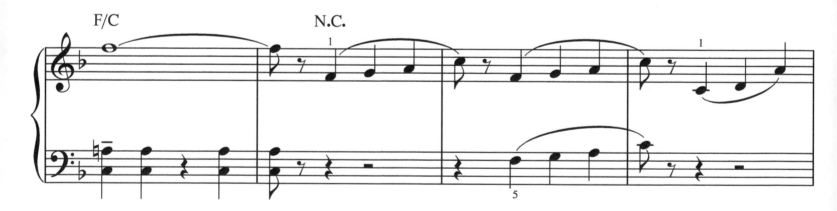

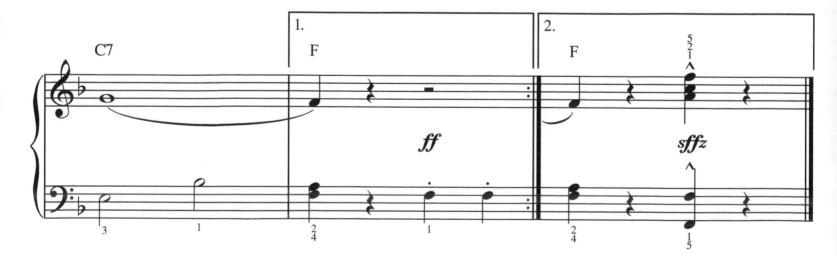

YANKEE DOODLE

Traditional
Arranged by Phillip Keveren

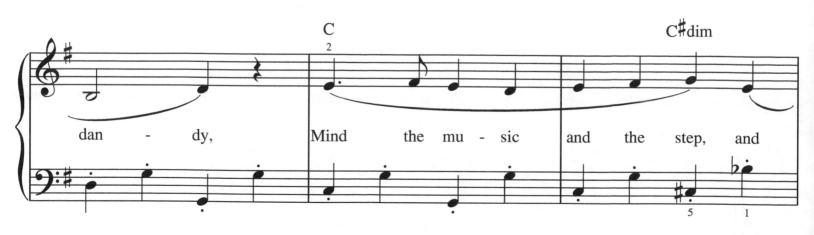

dan - dy, Mind the mu - sic and the step, and

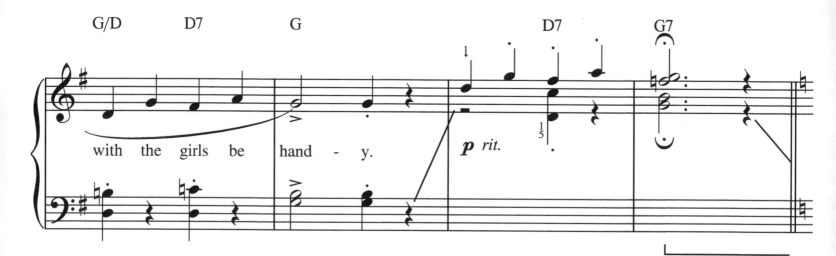

with the girls be hand - y.

There we saw a thou - sand men, as rich as Squi - re

Da - vid. And what they was - ted ev - 'ry day, I

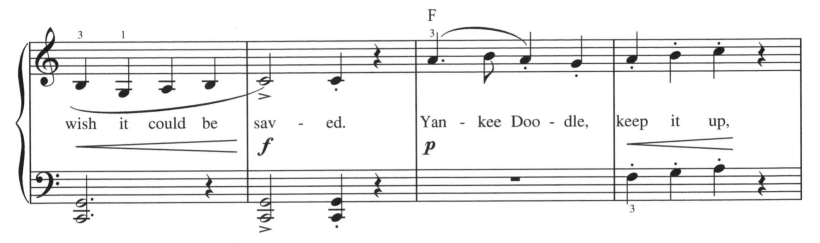

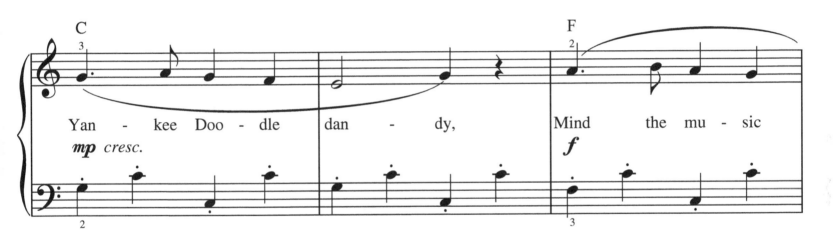

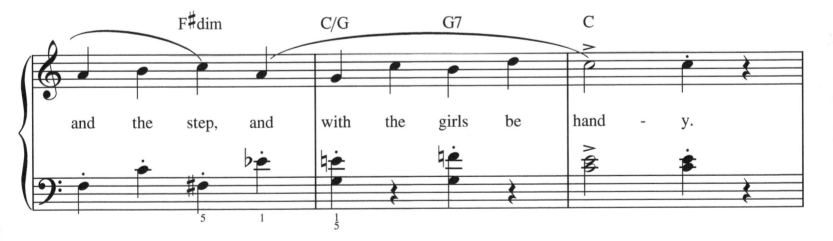

WASHINGTON POST MARCH

By JOHN PHILIP SOUSA
Arranged by Phillip Keveren

Spirited March (in two)

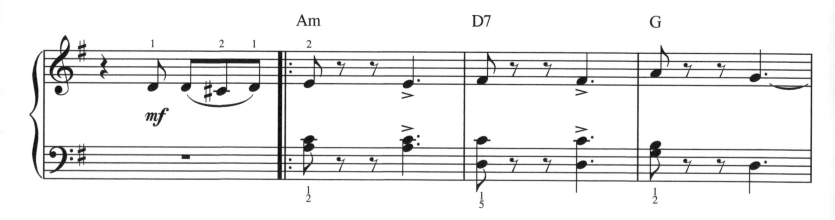

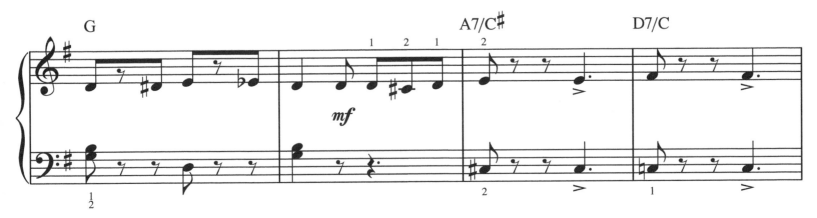

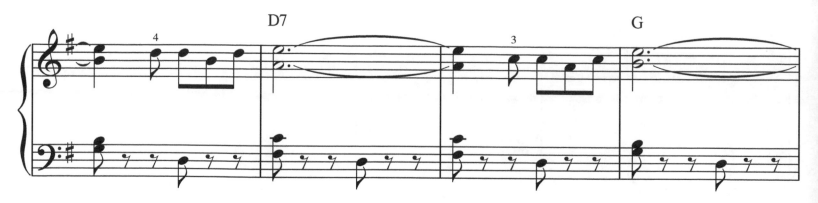

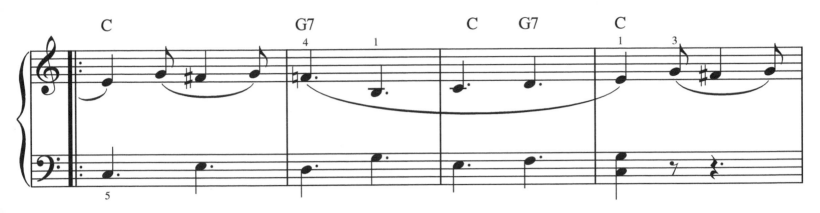

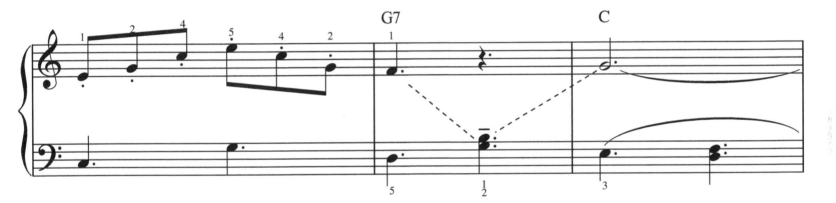

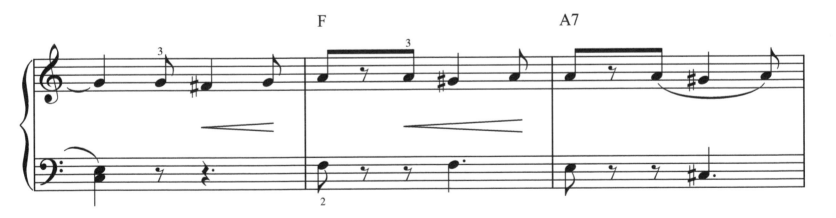

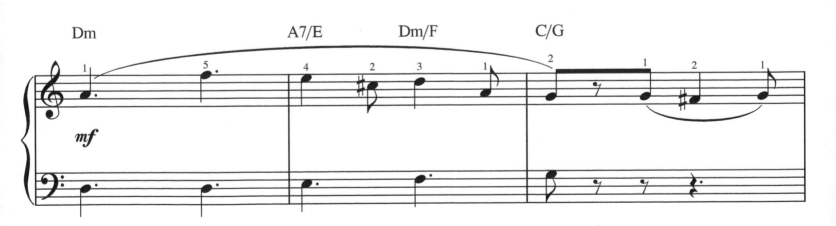

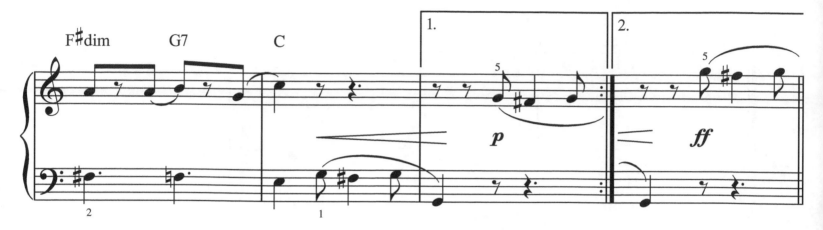

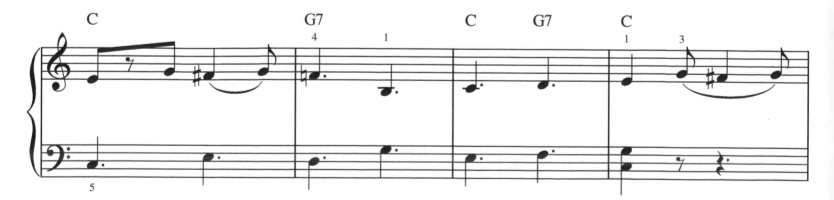

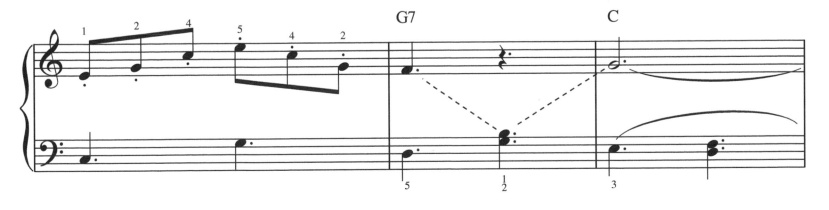

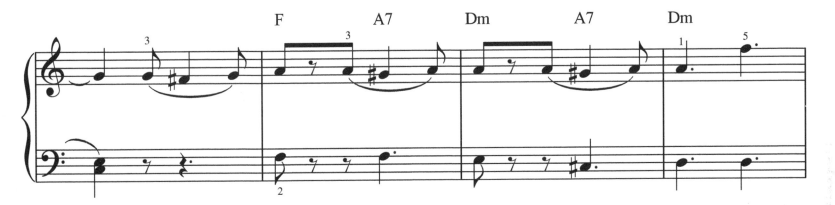

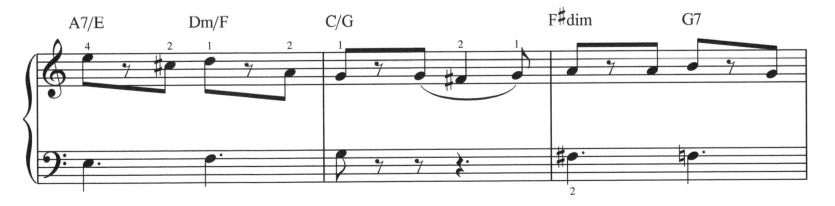

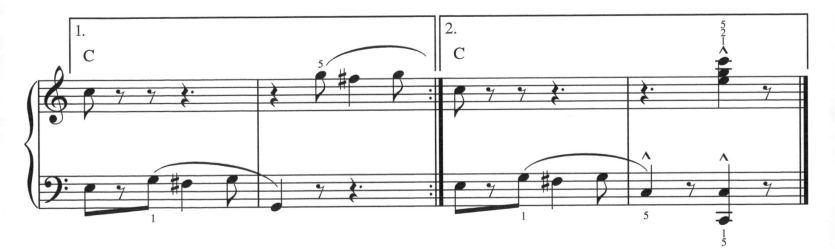

YANKEE DOODLE BOY

from LITTLE JOHNNY JONES

Words and Music by GEORGE M. COHAN
Arranged by Phillip Keveren

March tempo

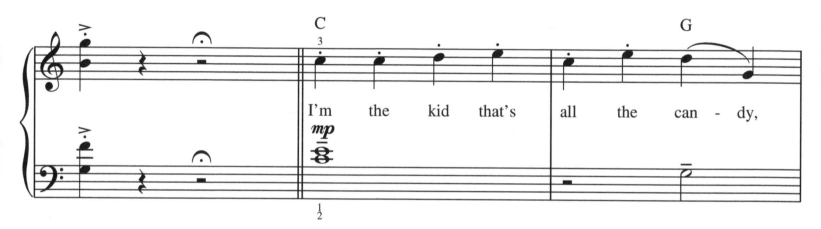

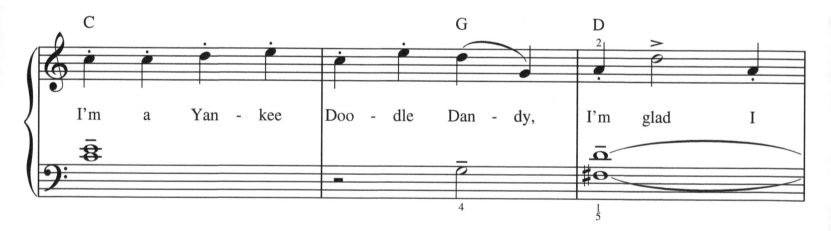

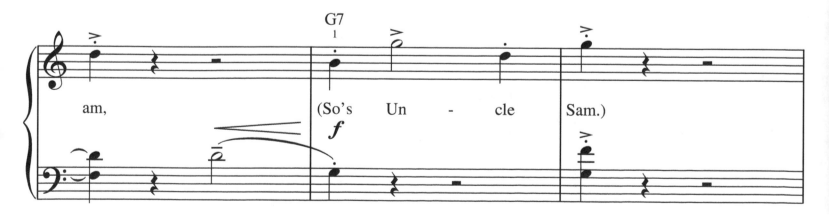

I'm a real live Yan - kee Doo - dle, Made my name and

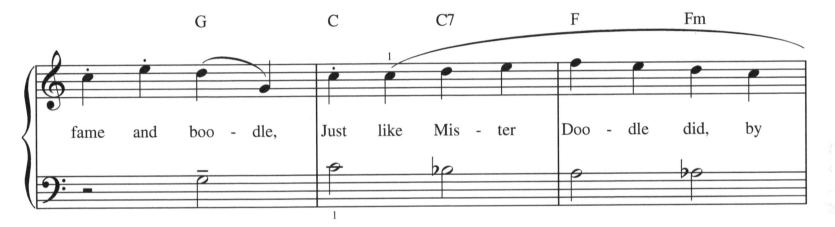

fame and boo - dle, Just like Mis - ter Doo - dle did, by

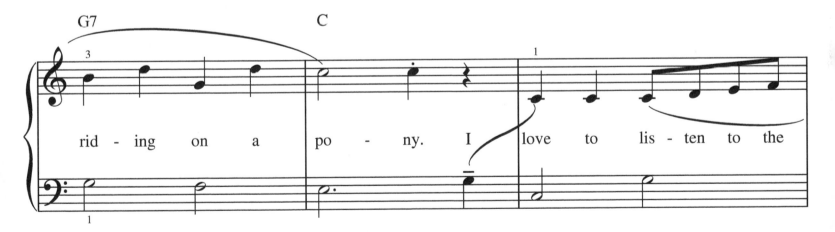

rid - ing on a po - ny. I love to lis - ten to the

Dix - ey strain, "I long to see the girl I left be - hind me,"

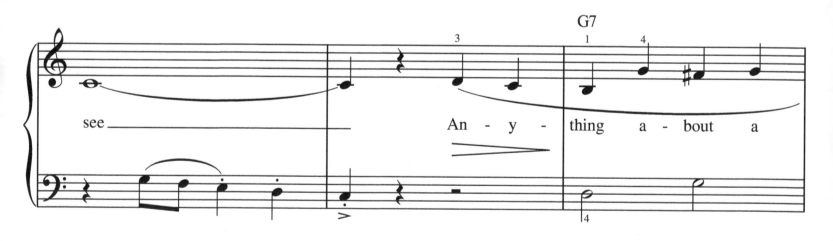

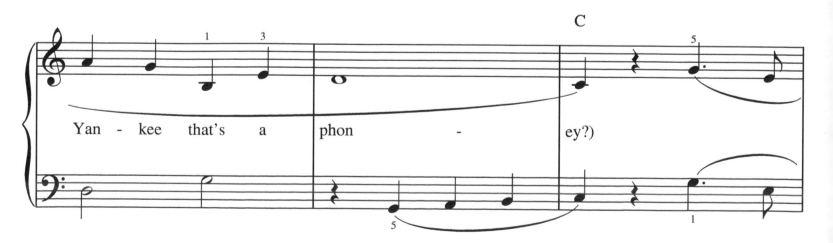

molto rit.

F#dim

C7   F

f

mf-f *a tempo*

I'm   a   Yan - kee   Doo - dle

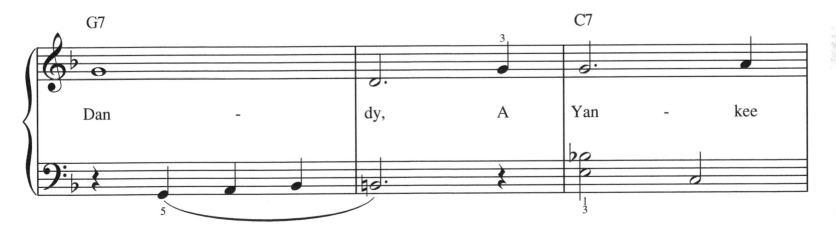

G7   C7

Dan   -   dy,   A   Yan - kee

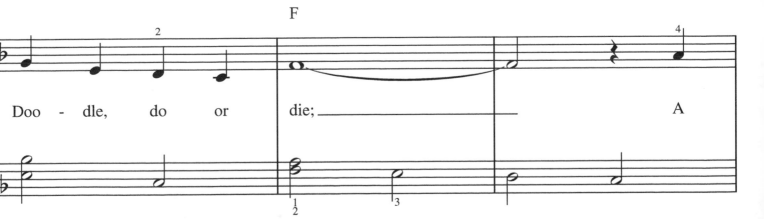

F

Doo - dle,   do or   die;_____   A

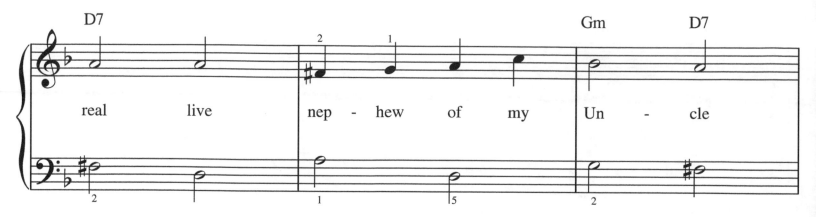

real   live   nep - hew of my   Un   -   cle

Sam's,   Born   on   the   Fourth of   Ju -

ly.   I've   got   a

Yan - kee   Doo - dle   sweet   -   heart,

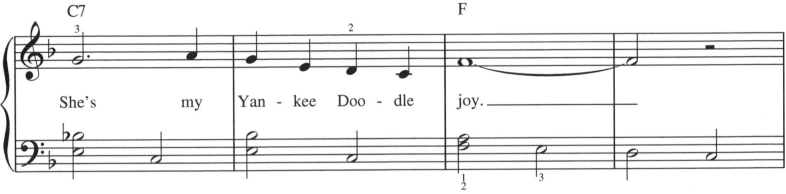

She's my Yan - kee Doo - dle joy. _____

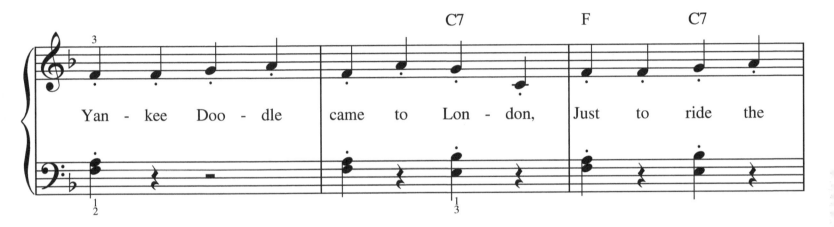

Yan - kee Doo - dle came to Lon - don, Just to ride the

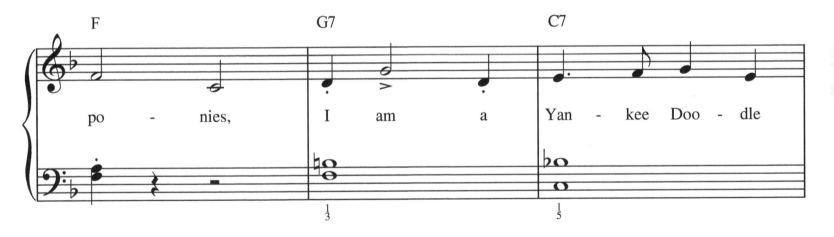

po - nies, I am a Yan - kee Doo - dle

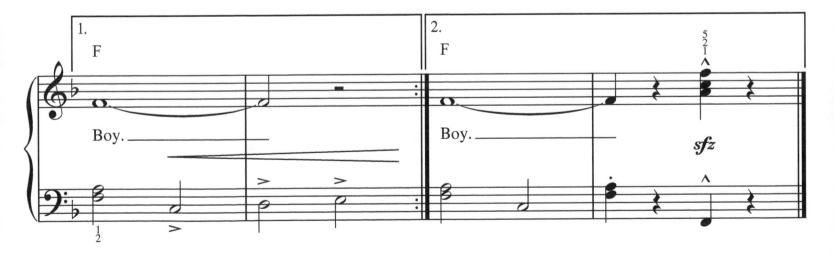

1. Boy. _____

2. Boy. _____

YOU'RE A GRAND OLD FLAG

from GEORGE M!

Words and Music by GEORGE M. COHAN
Arranged by Phillip Keveren

March tempo

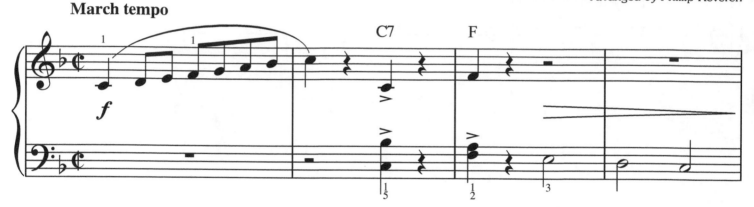

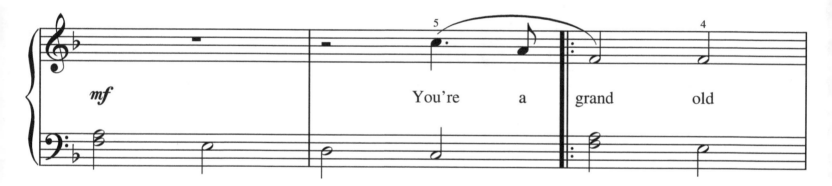

You're a grand old

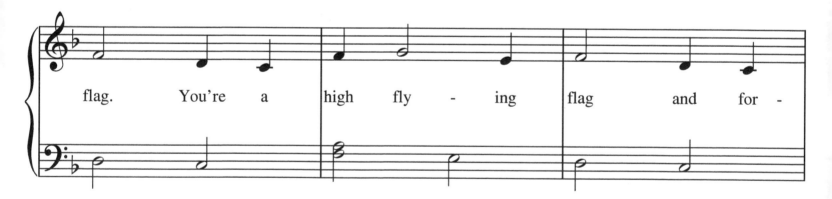

flag. You're a high fly - ing flag and for -

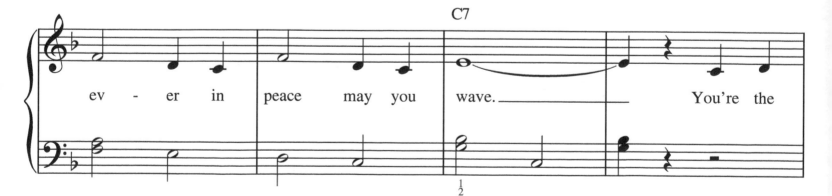

ev - er in peace may you wave. You're the

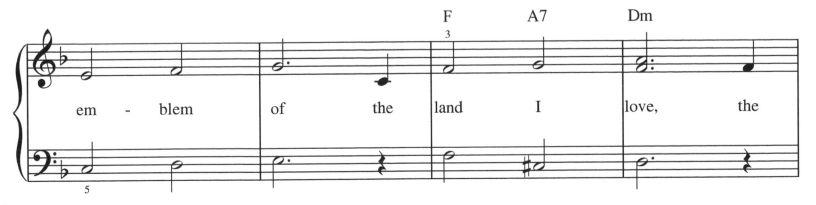

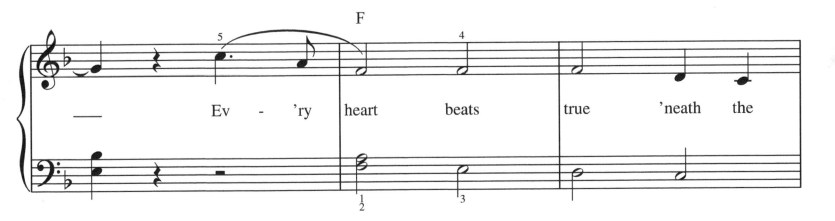

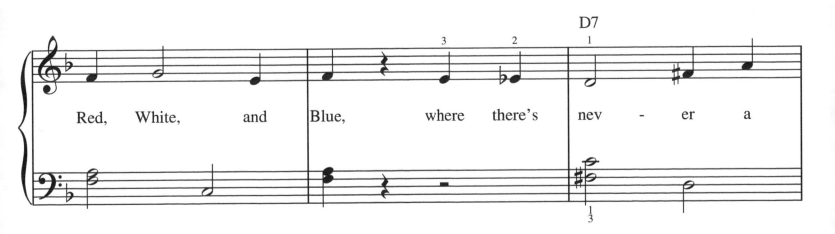

64

boast   or   brag. _____   But   should   auld   ac -

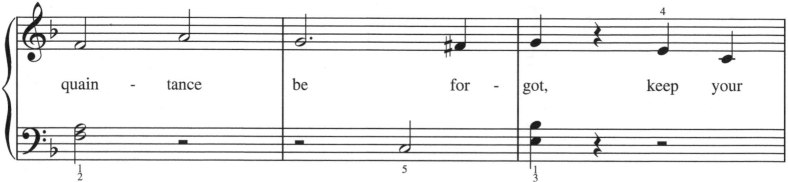

quain - tance   be   for - got,   keep   your

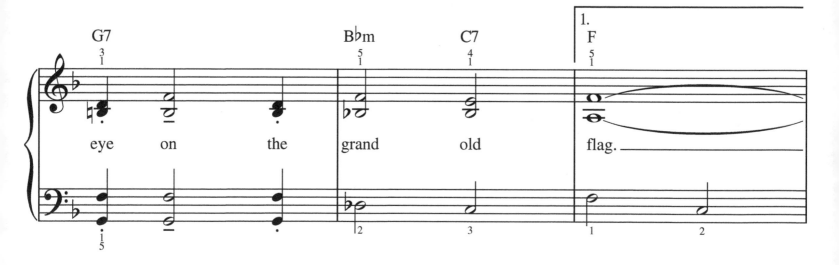

eye   on   the   grand   old   flag. _____

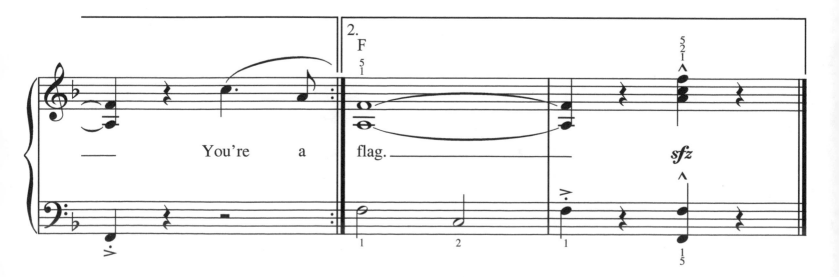

_____   You're   a   flag. _____